BRITISH
TROLLEYBUSES
IN COLOUR

BRITISH
TROLLEYBUSES
IN COLOUR
– THE LAST DECADE 1961-1972 –

MALCOLM KEEPING
AND JOHN BISHOP

FONTHILL

Fonthill Media Limited
www.fonthillmedia.com
office@fonthillmedia.com

First published in the UK 2015

British Library Cataloguing in Publication Data:
A catalogue record for this book is available from the British Library

ISBN 978-1-78155-450-0

Typeset in 10pt on 13pt Sabon
Printed and bound by CPI Group (UK) Ltd, Croydon, CR0 4YY

Contents

Introduction

Mention the word 'trolleybus' today and to the uninitiated the response will most likely be, 'Do they run on rails?' One must remember the last trolleybus in the UK operated in 1972, so one would have to be fifty or more to accurately remember them in service. To the tram enthusiast it is a vehicle to be despised, as it did for the much loved tramcar, and with it its relative quietness and comfort. To the professional brethren it was neither a tram or a diesel bus, 'neither one thing nor another', but merely a hybrid until the final demise sixty-one years after the tram's introduction in the UK.

The trolleybuses were first introduced to the travelling public in 1911 by both the Bradford and Leeds Corporations following earlier demonstration lines in the UK and in Europe, with the centenary being celebrated in 2011 in the UK. They were indeed crude machines, very much like the petrol buses of the time; however, with electricity provided for by the municipal companies, they benefited from substantially cheaper fuel. Initially the trolleybuses were more often introduced as feeders to the tramways, being substantially cheaper to install than a fully-fledged tramway (which of course was the mainstay of many towns and cities in the early part of the twentieth century). The early trolleybuses were basic, using tram controllers but operated on the road rather than track. They would collect their power from two suspended wires via trolley poles instead of the single trolley pole. Manufacturers in the second decade were principally Cedes Stoll, Railless Electric Traction, Tilling Stevens, and Straker Clough, to name just four. As time progressed, the Government in the early 1930s recommended the withdrawal of tram systems. Operators were faced with tram infrastructure starting to wear out, while management were faced with either the potentially huge cost of track renewal or replacing the tram with the trolleybus—a swift, silent, reliable, and elegant machine. In many cases the latter was the sensible option, especially when the municipal systems produced their own electricity and the electric feeder cables were already in place for the seemingly unpopular tram. While the UK did not pioneer the trolleybus, it soon overtook other countries, and soon the number of vehicles in service at home and abroad indicated our manufacturing ability. When the tram was replaced by the trolleybus, the travelling public must have thought it was enjoying 'comfort beyond belief' on first hearing its trademark sound. The earlier trolleybus manufacturers were soon overtaken by the then household names of Leyland Motors, Associated Equipment Company (AEC), Karrier, Sunbeam, Garrett, Ransomes, Simms and Jefferies, English Electric, and Guy Motors, and by other companies who built experimental vehicles—namely Bristol and Thornycroft, to name but two.

After the Second World War, the few municipal operators who still operated trams found the infrastructure in poor condition through lack of maintenance during the hostilities. Therefore, the trolleybus became a diesel bus, which by now had become far more reliable than its pre-war predecessors. But the tide had not entirely turned yet, with new trolleybuses being purchased to replace pre-war examples. Glasgow Corporation replaced some of their tram routes in 1949 with new trolleybuses, albeit on a comparatively small scale. Confronted with diminishing markets, Leyland Motors and AEC joined to form British United Traction (BUT) with Sunbeam, Crossley, and Daimler—the post-war manufacturers. (By now Karrier was part of Sunbeam, who in turn were part of Guy Motors.)

This period was short-lived. In the 1950s, the tide turned against the trolleybus following nationalisation of the electricity companies. No longer would they enjoy cheap electricity produced by the local authorities—the cost of extensions spiralled, and the diesel bus grew cheaper. There were a few company-operated trolleybuses outside municipal control and these were among the first to withdraw their trolleybuses. These companies were the Balfour Beatty Company (in Llanelli, South Wales, Nottingham, and Derby), the British Electric Traction Company (Hastings and Mexborough), and finally the nationalised Brighton Hove & District operation. The final curtain for the trolleybus came when in the mid-1950s London Transport—by far the largest system in the UK and the world at that time—announced the abandonment policy, which claimed the last capital city service trolleybus on 8 May 1962. Even the Suez Crisis in 1956 and Britain's subsequent oil predicament did not delay the trolleybus's decline.

Both authors were brought up in the seaside town of Brighton, where the trolleybuses were loved by the citizens for their efficient ability to swiftly climb the hills with enviable ease. Upon withdrawal of Brighton's last trolleybus in June 1961, the decision was made by the authors to cover the remaining systems in the UK. By using colour transparency film and cine film, the variety of colour and operating conditions would remain an everlasting memory.

The Government's policy of abandonment proceeded over the next eleven years. On 26 March 1972, the City of Bradford finally switched off the power of the last trolleybus to run on British roads at Thornbury Depot—a sad day indeed. While various proposals have been forthcoming, even that of a test line in Doncaster in 1985, no profitable vehicles have entered service since then. The final curtain has not apparently come down as yet: one of the pioneering cities, Leeds, now has firm proposals for a trolleybus installation within the next four years. A scheme has even been proposed in Oxford Street, London, to install trolleybuses rather than a tram line. We hold our breath in anticipation of the last proposal; it suggests to us that the 'age of the trolleybus' is far from over, or forgotten.

Those who still remember the trolleybus frequently ask why, then remark, 'They were so smooth and quiet,' 'They were so fast,' 'They were so quick on the hills'—although some would say they were the proverbial 'silent death'! None would say anything about the overhead, for when neatly installed and maintained, it was hardly noticeable.

The foresight of many enthusiasts, especially the late Michael Dare, means that we are fortunately able to witness the majesty and swiftness of the trolleybus in action today: at Sandtoft Trolleybus Museum near Doncaster, the East Anglia Transport Museum at Carlton Colville (near Lowestoft), the Black Country Museum at Dudley, and the North of England Open Air Museum in Durham.

John Bishop and Malcolm Keeping
October 2014

1

Trolleybuses in Everyday Service

Ashton-under-Lyne Corporation

Five Crossley 'Empires' were delivered to Ashton-under-Lyne in 1950. Seen passing under the railway bridge at Stalybridge Station is No. 80 (LTC 774), with only yards to go before arriving at Market Street and the terminus of routes 216 and 218 on 13 July 1964. No. 80 was withdrawn in October 1964 and can still be seen in preservation. An interesting fact in Stalybridge: the overhead was owned and maintained by the local authority, however they were never to operate trolleybuses. (*Malcolm Keeping*)

The final delivery of trolleybuses for Ashton-under-Lyne came in 1956 when eight BUT 9612Ts arrived with locally built bodies by S. H. Bond from Wythenshawe just outside Manchester. These vehicles maintained Ashton's commitment to the joint operation with Manchester until the end of December 1966, when both systems closed. No. 89 (YTE 828) is seen in July 1964 at Stalybridge before departure to Manchester. (*John Bishop*)

We conclude our look at Ashton-under-Lyne at the depot in Mosley Road on 13 July 1964 with two types of vehicles: a Roe-bodied Sunbeam No. 61 and Bond-bodied BUT No. 82. The two trolleybuses are waiting to take up duty for the rush hour. It is well to point out that No. 61 (FTE 645) was a wartime utility vehicle and was re-bodied by Roe of Leeds in 1958. When one considers the external condition of these vehicles, it is hard to believe that within two years all this would be but a memory and later still Ashton Corporation would be part of the Passenger Transport Executive. (*Malcolm Keeping*)

Belfast Corporation

The first large order for trolleybuses were for eighty-eight locally built Harkness-bodied AEC 664Ts, delivered between 1940 and 1943 to commence the tram withdrawal. They were delivered in blue and white, but after the hostilities the decision was made to change the livery to red and cream, a process which was to take two years. AEC No. 19 (FZ 7804) is seen in Donegall Square looking worse for wear in 1963. This was its twentieth and last year in service. (*John Bishop*)

After the war years, Belfast Corporation placed a large order with Guy Motors (numbered 143 to 186) for delivery between 1948 and 49. As with all orders the bodywork would be by the local coachbuilder, Harkness. No. 146 (GZ 8510) is seen in Shore Road just about to negotiate the turning circle at Fort William the terminus for route 8. Fort William was perfect for the photographing of a moving vehicle, for it would have to slow down to minimize the risk of de-wirement and damage to the overhead wiring. (*Malcolm Keeping*)

The following order of Guy trolleybuses, Harkness-bodied BUT 9641Ts (numbered 187 to 234) were delivered between 1948 and 1954. In this view, No. 206 (GZ 8570) has the same design as the previous Guy BTX chassis dating from 1950 and is seen in Whiterock Road with the backdrop of the Black Mountains on 6 July 1965. (*Malcolm Keeping*)

The last batch totalling twenty-four BUTs came in 1954 with more modern styling by Harkness. This is No. 212 (OZ 7314) in Donegall Place, where it is leaving on route 12 for Falls Road in June 1963. There are three sets of overhead wiring, allowing for greater flexibility for all services. (*John Bishop*)

The last vehicle to be delivered to Belfast was fleet number 246 (2206 OI), a Sunbeam F4A on a 30-foot-long chassis with Harkness bodywork not too dissimilar to the previous deliveries in 1954. It was hoped this would be the prelude to a new fleet of trolleybuses, however this was not to be. No. 246 is seen at the terminus of the long route to Glengormley from the city centre. Fortunately, this unique vehicle to Belfast is saved and was used in the final closing ceremony on 12 May 1968. (*John Bishop*)

Bournemouth Corporation Transport

After various trial vehicles, Bournemouth Corporation decided on the Sunbeam MS2 three-axle chassis with dual entrance bodywork by Park Royal. Our view of No. 208 (ALJ 64) typifies the design, which remained unaltered. The body had two staircases with a conventional open rear platform and an exit door at the front. This vehicle was originally fleet numbered 88 when delivered in 1934, but renumbered 208 with others between 1959 and 1960, bringing it in line with newer vehicles and catering for withdrawal of similar vehicles. This vehicle was an incredible twenty-nine years old when it finally retired and was withdrawn in 1963. The location is the Triangle, where many an off-peak trolleybus and motor bus could be found waiting for the evening rush hour. (*Malcolm Keeping*)

During 1957 and 1958, three of the ageing Park Royal Sunbeam MS2s were converted to open-top, whereupon they had their front staircases removed along with the folding doors, bringing the lower saloon to a conventional layout. The upper deck was completely removed down to window level, a steel gantry was fixed to the original body uprights and this structure supported the trolley base and poles. This whole re-construction was very reminiscent of the Hastings and District Guy BTX trolleybus, which were some thirty years older. The three vehicles were numbered 200 to 202 with No. 200 being the ex-157, No. 201 the ex-160, and 202 the ex-112. They were used on round-the-town circular tours numbered 39. Alas the route was withdrawn in September 1963. These vehicles were popular with private groups and this view of No. 202 ex-112 was one such occasion, taken at Bournemouth Pier on Sunday 20 April 1969 for the closure ceremony. (*John Bishop*)

After the war the Bournemouth system was extended way beyond the extremities of the trams they replaced, therefore it was necessary to purchase new vehicles. Twenty-four Weymann-bodied BUT 9641Ts were purchased and numbered 200 to 223 (KLJ 334 to 357). These were later re-numbered 234 to 257 in 1958–9, thus the registration numbers coincided with the fleet number. Bournemouth Square is the setting for No. 249 (KLJ 349), a Weymann-bodied BUT 9641T on a hot bank holiday in August in 1963 on route 22 for Christchurch. This nearside view displays the dual door arrangement and three axles which as outlined earlier, the standard configuration for Bournemouth Corporation. Worthy of note is the concise destination information and the white finishes at the end of the trolley booms. (*John Bishop*)

Mention Bournemouth trolleybuses and the turntable at the Christchurch Terminus will come into conversation—it still exists today. Since the demise of the trolleybuses in 1969 (of which more later), this area has been built over and the turntable is still at the rear of the buildings. In happier times, on 19 April 1969—the penultimate day of trolleybus operation—No. 272 (WRU 272) has just come onto the turntable and having turned and re-poled will set off for the journey back to Bournemouth town centre. Thirty-nine Weymann-bodied Sunbeam MF2Bs were delivered, of which No. 272 is here depicted, representing the first batch of twenty delivered between 1958 and 1959. Regretfully, the condition of No. 272 does not reflect the usual presentation of Bournemouth Corporation vehicles and was clearly at the end of its life. (*John Bishop*)

When this view was taken on 14 June 1964, the Weymann-bodied Sunbeam MF2B No. 300 (300 LJ) was only two years old and sparkled in the bright sunshine when seen travelling from Christchurch to Bournemouth on the route 22. This vehicle was one of only ten trolleybuses to receive reversed registration numbers (nine in Bournemouth and one in Belfast in 1958). This batch of vehicles should have amounted to ten, however a disastrous fire broke out at the Weymann factory in Addlestone, Surrey, damaging one of the ten vehicles of the batch beyond feasible repair. Alas, the tenth one of the batch never did appear, as the tide had by then turned against the trolleybus, even at this supposed safe haven. Upon the impending closure of the system, this particular vehicle travelled up to Walsall in January 1969 for experimental rebuilding as a one-man operated bi-mode vehicle; however, this venture was concluded before the work was completed. (*John Bishop*)

16

As representative of the few second-hand vehicles ever purchased by Bournemouth Corporation in later years, BUT No. 288 (HUF 45), ex Brighton Corporation 45, now fleet number 288, was one of seven that arrived from Brighton in 1959 upon closure of the first stage of trolleybuses, with four from Brighton Corporation and three from the Brighton, Hove & District Company. This view at the Triangle in July 1963 shows No. 288 among fellow Weymann products with an ex Brighton Hove & District behind, and to the right a Weymann-bodied Leyland Titan PD2. All the Brighton BUTs would be withdrawn by November 1965 after six years' service with Bournemouth Corporation. (*Malcolm Keeping*)

'The end is nigh'. It is Saturday 19 April 1969, and those who were there will remember it was one of those cold evenings, but at least it was not raining! No. 278 (YLJ 278) was picked as the illuminated trolleybus to operate for the last week, emblazoned with the legend 'Last week of Bournemouth Trolleybuses', 'BCT 1933–1969', and the County Borough of Bournemouth coat of arms. (*John Bishop*)

Bradford City Transport

The trolleybus was always popular for their longevity of life, especially the chassis. Thus, many operators often re-bodied them, and Bradford Corporation were in essence 'the experts' in this field: they went to various body manufacturers with numerous pre-war and post-war chassis acquired over the years. In the city centre (which had already seen rebuilding), we see No. 652 (CAK 652), an AEC 661T about to depart in August 1962 on the route 25 to Saltaire before the severing of cross-town services. No. 652 gained its new Crossley body in March 1952 and was finally withdrawn in 1963. (*John Bishop*)

No. 678 (CAK 678) was a Karrier E4 originally delivered with a Weymann body and entered service in September 1938. In March 1952 it was re-bodied by Crossley, remaining in service until October 1963. When captured on camera on 1 June 1963, No. 678 only had five months' service before withdrawal. Here No. 678 is seen on route 39 between Lidget Green and the city centre, which was basically one of the short workings of route 37. (*Malcolm Keeping*)

All the utility vehicles were re-bodied over a period of five years beginning in 1956, when the first twenty were fitted with new East Lancs. and rear-entrance bodies with platform doors, and the remainder with front-entrance bodies. Depicted are two such Karrier W vehicles at Tong Cemetery: the lead vehicle, No. 709 (DKY 709) with front entrance body, is to return to the depot, while the rear vehicle, No. 727 (DKY 727), is a rear-entrance vehicle bound for the city on route 18. Note the white Bond three-wheeler with fibre glass body behind No. 709—so popular in the sixties. (*Malcolm Keeping*)

Rear views are rare, but in this view we see the use of trolley retrievers on No. 712 (DKY712). This was one of a small number of trolleybuses experimentally fitted with trolley retrievers, but this policy was not successful and not pursued despite its use abroad. No. 712 is seen on route 6 on the Thornton Road in July 1963; at the time it was still sporting its rear bumpers. Just note the deserted road, unheard of today. (*Malcolm Keeping*)

The years 1949 and 1951 saw two small batches of new BUT 9611Ts arrive, which was a first from this manufacturer for Bradford Corporation. No. 743 (EKU 743) was from the first batch of twelve, with Roe bodywork; it entered service in December 1949. During their working life some of the class were stored for short periods, while others were used as driver training vehicles, however all returned later for full passenger service. The view is Bradford Moor terminal point for route 30 until November 1962. This particular vehicle fortunately was preserved and never made it to the scrapyard. (*John Bishop*)

No. 753 (FKU 753) formed part of the second batch of eight new BUT 9611Ts with Weymann bodies. These were destined to be the last new trolleybuses purchased by Bradford Corporation in 1950–51 by virtue of the availability of good serviceable vehicles being made elsewhere as systems closed down. This photograph was taken on the Buttershaw Estate on 15 March 1968. Note the very unusual, small extra window inserted in the nearside of the cab—presumably to give the driver better visibility of the kerb. This route would remain open until 31 July 1971. (*Malcolm Keeping*)

It would become the practice to re-body vehicles when purchased second-hand, however a number of trolleybuses did enter service with their original bodywork. One example was the small batch of eight East-Lancs.-bodied BUT 9611Ts from St Helens in 1959. Dating from 1950–51, these were very similar to the ones being re-bodied and overhauled before entering service. Here we see No. 796 (BDJ 84), ex No. 384, in the St Helens fleet at 5 Lane Ends, returning to the city on 11 October 1964. (*Malcolm Keeping*)

With the chassis dating from the war years in 1942, we see ex Notts & Derby AEC No. 594 (HNU 972) with its new East Lancs. body. It looks pristine outside the Midland Hotel, Foster Square, in July 1963. At this stage Foster Square was undergoing massive reconstruction, and as a result the cross-town services were severed and the route 24 terminated on temporary wiring. (*Malcolm Keeping*)

Photographed on a bright sunny day, we see No. 809 (BDY 799), one of twelve Sunbeam Ws purchased from Hastings (Maidstone & District) in 1959. Ten of the batch acquired had bodywork by Park Royal and two by Weymann. In this view we see a Park Royal example at the terminus of route 37 at Clayton, the driver, and his conductor, complete with Setright ticket machine. Upon acquisition the vehicle had little alteration to its original bodywork since entering service, except for the destination screen which was rebuilt. No. 809 only remained in service for two years. (*Malcolm Keeping*)

On a sunny day in August 1963 at Thornbury Depot are two fine examples of ex Notts & Derby BUT 9611Ts. These were purchased at the closure of their system in 1953 and were among a small number of vehicles which retained their original bodies and were not rebuilt. The one nearest the camera, No. 773 (NNU 237) has received the rebuilt Bradford standard destination layout and also the larger square grill on the front panel. To the left No. 761 (NNU 225) is in virtually original condition. Both vehicles were withdrawn on the same day, 31 October 1963. We could not close this caption without drawing your attention to the classic example of the tram depot design, now sadly demolished. (*John Bishop*)

Hard to imagine this was once a single-deck trolleybus in Darlington. East-Lancs.-bodied Karrier W No. 785 (GHN 403) was one of a number purchased from Darlington Corporation between 1954 and 1957, when a total of twenty-four were received of which only nine were re-bodied the remainder being dismantled for spares. No. 785 had two lives in Bradford being the only one to enter passenger service in its original utility single deck form as number T403 for one year then re-bodied in keeping with the rest of the class. In this view taken in the mid-sixties, No. 785 takes the sun at Wibsey Terminus while the driver and conductor sit on the bench. Note the bus stop which has the writing 'BCT TROLLEYBUS STOP'—once one of hundreds throughout the city, but now just a memory. (*John Bishop*)

A late example of the re-bodying programme was No. 835 (LHN 785), which started life in the fleet of Darlington Corporation as their BUT 9611T No. 73. In 1952, after only three years, it was sold to Doncaster Corporation to become their No. 383; in 1959 it was sold to Bradford. The original East Lancs. body was scrapped and by August 1962 No. 835 re-entered service, as seen. By 1 June 1971 it was finally withdrawn from service, along with the rest of its class. Our view of No. 835 was taken on 1 June 1963 at Saltaire, as it was ready to return to Bradford city centre. Glimpsed in the far background is the Saltaire Depot, which still exists today as a restaurant. (*Malcolm Keeping*)

Brighton Corporation

When they replaced trams, Brighton trolleybuses ranked among the best appointed vehicles in Britain: the Weymann body was well proportioned and the interiors were to a very high standard, with alhambrinal ceilings on both decks, interior lights mounted in chrome frames with glass covers, and even the interior advertisement were mounted in polished wooden frames. No. 15 (FUF 15) shows the handsome lines of the bodywork here on 20 March 1961, in the Old Steine close to the Palace Pier (now Brighton Pier). The Old Steine was the terminus point for the tram system and in 1939 became the trolleybus terminal point. Interestingly, the railings in front of the vehicle were placed there in tram days and only in recent years have they finally been replaced. This location in its heyday would be thronged with people, especially on holidays, in contrast to this view, which seems to be begging for passengers! (*Malcolm Keeping*)

This view shows the steep nature of Brighton's streets, where the trolleybuses were able to extol their virtue by swiftly climbing the hills. Brighton Corporation's No. 31 (FUF 31) is about to descend the last part of Ditchling Road on route 26 from Hollingbury to Old Steine. There were a number of locations in Brighton where the coasting brake would be applied, usually at a conveniently positioned bus stop. With three months to go on 26 March 1961, No. 31 would have to take extra care over the power and section isolators above. (*Malcolm Keeping*)

Cardiff Corporation

Cardiff commenced trolleybus operations in 1941 and took delivery of ten handsome three-axle double-deck AEC 664Ts bodied by Northern Counties. They had various liveries, from wartime grey to streamlined livery, before settling down to the standard livery seen on No. 207 (CKG 197) at Victoria Park on a short working route 8 on 27 June 1962. Withdrawal for this class was long and painful by virtue of them being used for illuminations at Christmas time. Regretfully, a colour view does not appear to exist as far as we can ascertain. Final withdrawal came in 1965. We are fortunate that No. 203 has survived into preservation, where it has appeared in the various forms of livery worn by the class since first being delivered. (*Malcolm Keeping*)

In the previous photograph reference is made to the use of the AECs for illuminations, and the light sockets can be seen in this view of the rear offside of No. 201 (CKG 191). In front in the outside parking area of the depot are further trolleybuses of the same class, also with light sockets. Small and lighter trolley heads were developed by Cardiff Corporation to lessen the number of de-wirements. These trolley heads would remain unique to this fleet. (*John Bishop*)

One of the last sections of wiring to be installed in 1965 past the City Hall provides the attractive backdrop for this view of No. 213 (DBO 473), posed on a private hire tour of the system in the summer of 1967. No. 213 was one of twenty BUT 9641Ts with East Lancs. bodies delivered in 1948. The class underwent rebuilding throughout their lives. Originally fitted with a rear entrance and forward exit, they became conventional with the 'exit' sealed, the destination boxes rubber-mounted, new headlamps, and simplified livery which dispensed with lining out—the wings were painted with the standard livery rather than black. (*John Bishop*)

The pier head tram route was converted into a bus route in 1946, but then trolleybuses won the day and replaced the buses! It was necessary to use single-deck trolley vehicles due to a very low bridge and one from the first batch of East Lancs., single-deck BUTs, and No. 239 dating from 1949, is seen here in Bute Street. Five were delivered and this was followed by a sixth BUT 9641T in 1955, re-affirming the city's confidence in the trolleybus. No. 239 is just about to turn at the reverser so that it may travel back from whence it came. (*Malcolm Keeping*)

The next batch of double-deck trolleybuses to be delivered is exemplified by No. 247 (EBO 904), seen here at Roath Park to the north of the city on 29 March 1964. Delivered in 1949, the vehicle is an East-Lancs.-bodied BUT 9641T finished off by Bruce Coachworks, a local company. From this view we can see how the bead lining on the body and wings were black before the livery was simplified, and the destination box in its original design. No. 247 would be withdrawn in March 1966. (*John Bishop*)

No. 284 (KBO 957) is from the last batch of BUT 9641Ts with East Lancs. bodies—a reaffirmation of faith in the three-axle BUT chassis in 1955. Seen in Green Farm Road Estate at Ely on 27 June 1962, No. 284 was still only seven years old and when delivered had the conventional one entrance at the rear rather than the dual-door layout (exit at the front and entrance at the rear). This route was an extension far beyond the original tram route, at Victoria Park on 8 May 1955, and the last to be withdrawn in 1970 on 11 January. (*Malcolm Keeping*)

Derby Corporation

No. 171 (RC 8471) represents fifteen Sunbeam Ws acquired between 1944 and early 1946. The first two, Nos. 171 and 172, were bodied by Weymann, whereas the rest, Nos. 173 to 185, were to the relaxed specification by Park Royal. When delivered, none had route number boxes, lined out with gold lining and khaki roofs. Nos. 171 and 172 were to full wartime specifications, with steel panels, wooden framework, and wooden seats—nevertheless, they would be in service until 1965. In this view taken on 16 July 1963, No. 171 is laying over at Midland Station, out of service with its poles down. Fortunately No. 172 was saved for preservation by the late Michael Dare and can be seen at the Sandtoft Trolleybus Museum near Doncaster in full wartime specification. (*Malcolm Keeping*)

This is a classic photograph of a 'relaxed utility': No. 180 (RC 8880) in its last year of service in 1964, seen turning into Ascot Drive after service. No. 180 represents the thirteen Sunbeam Ws acquired between 1945 and early 1946 with bodies by Park Royal. Fortunately No. 175 of this batch of vehicles is preserved at Sandtoft Trolleybus Museum for us to enjoy today. (*John Bishop*)

28

After the war years Derby Corporation set about replacing the ageing pre-war Guy trolleybuses in earnest, making its second generation of vehicles Sunbeam F4 chassis. The first batch of twenty were Brush-bodied, as depicted by No. 203 (ARC 503): here we see it in the early 1960s in the market place, as it negotiates the labyrinth of overhead on its way to Alvaston. The assembly room in the background should be familiar to those who have visited the Crich Tramway Village, as it is now situated at the terminus of the trams. (*John Bishop*)

The next batch to follow the Brush-bodied Sunbeam F4s were twenty vehicles bodied by Willowbrook, who took over the bodybuilding activities of Brush. These were delivered over 1952 and 1953 and would last until 1967, when the final trolleybus operated in Derby. In this view we see numerically the last of the batch No. 235 (DRC 235) on route 22 to Prince Charles Avenue and Morden Green in the west of the city. It is the summer of 1967. No. 235 waits in the lay-by for the classic AEC-articulated lorry to pass. (*John Bishop*)

29

The last order for trolleybuses was for eight Sunbeam F4As fitted with very smart, well-proportioned Roe-bodied Nos. 236 to 243, delivered between 1959 and 1960. These would signal the departure for the pre-war Daimler trolleybuses. On 25 June 1962, we see No. 239 (SCH 239) still looking smart close to the market place, on route 66 to Nottingham Road Cemetery. While one section at Cavendish had been withdrawn, no wholesale withdrawals had taken place. However, in 1962 the Nottingham Road route was closed. (*Malcolm Keeping*)

The location for this view is Nottingham Road Terminus, with No. 236 (SCH 236)'s destination screen set for the return journey via the city centre for Shelton Lock. This was the first of the batch of Roe-bodied Sunbeam F4As, and would see only eight years' service. Note the Barton AEC Regent V negotiating the roundabout. (*John Bishop*)

Doncaster Corporation

This trolleybus, No. 373 (CDT 625), is a Roe-bodied Karrier W which originally had a Brush utility body until July 1954. No. 373 is seen on 24 June 1962 at the end of the journey at Balby, the southernmost point on the Doncaster system. Had the proposed scheme gone through in the late 1920s, this would have been where the Rotherham and Doncaster systems connected. (*Malcolm Keeping*)

It has to be said that, in the latter days of Doncaster trolleybuses, they looked very alike with their new Roe bodies. However, the chassis certainly were not alike, being sourced from other operators who sold off their vehicles when taken out of service. In this instance, No. 387 (BHJ 898), seen at Wheatley Hills came from Southend Corporation in 1954, and by 1956 had a new body by Roe. (*John Bishop*)

In this view we are at the end of the Becket Road route, which was at the time of this photograph a relatively new extension, having been commissioned on 17 February 1958. No. 354 (FWX 902), a Sunbeam W with a Roe body was originally a single-deck trolleybus with Mexborough & Swinton as their No. 18. This scene was taken on 2 June 1963, six months before the closure. Because the body was relatively new it was removed and fitted to Leyland PD2 Titan 123, KDT 562, for further service. (*Malcolm Keeping*)

Glasgow Corporation

Glasgow was late in adopting the trolleybus in 1949 and a few routes were chosen for tram replacement. Although the fleet grew to nearly 200 strong, the public were never to hold them in the same affection as their beloved trams. The route shown on No. TB31 (FYS 731), the 102 from Riddrie to Polmadie, was the first, followed by 101 from Royston Road to Cathedral Street. The routes were much altered as time went on; needless to say the seeds were sown. The BUT/MCCW vehicle depicted, No. TB31, was one of the first vehicles to arrive in 1949. The livery worn was its fourth and last variant. (*Malcolm Keeping*)

Seen at Hampden Park Depot on 11 July 1963 is one of the thirty-strong batch of Daimler CTME trolleybuses, with MCCW bodywork No. TD28 (FYS 762). The time on the depot clock is 3.30 p.m.; the vehicle is preparing to leave the depot for the school journey and help out with the rush hour. These Daimlers were the second batch of trolleybuses delivered to Glasgow from 1950 to 1951. They were the only example of the London class Q1 style of MCCW body to be fitted to a different chassis manufacturer other than the BUT. The class were withdrawn over the period from 1958 to 1964, giving some of these vehicles a very short working life in the city. This vehicle, however, survived to be repainted in the final livery. (*Malcolm Keeping*)

The dark-stained blocks which make up central Glasgow set the scene for No. TG10 (FYS 785). The fleet numbering would tell you the vehicle is a trolleybus, and the next letter the manufacturer, which in this case is Guy Motors—although this is a Sunbeam F4! In fairness, Guy were the manufacturer and Sunbeam the subsidiary. The body in this instance is a Weymann and wears the third-stage livery which many of us remember with affection. No. TG10 was delivered in 1953 and would last only twelve years being withdrawn in 1965. (*Malcolm Keeping*)

In 1951 Glasgow Corporation purchased No. TBS 1, a BUT RETB1 with Weymann bodywork. Of all the Glasgow vehicles this must hold the most interesting history, having been part of a failed 'Pay as You Enter' experiment. The passengers would board the bus at the rear, pay the seated conductor, and alight at the front entrance at the end of his or her journey. While there were only twenty-six seats, there was provision for forty standing; in any case the experiment was never successful. Originally given the fleet number TB35 following on from the double-deck BUTs, it was renumbered TBS 1 (i.e. 'Trolleybus BUT Single-decker'). The rear entrance was taken away and fitted in the centre and would bear a similarity with the rest of the class delivered later in 1953. They were to prove elusive to film on the road and it was pure luck to capture No. TBS1 when the conductor just about to change the frog above on the traction pole. (*John Bishop*)

Glasgow took into stock ten short BUT RETB1 trolleybuses with East Lancashire bodies numbered (TBS2-11) in 1953. The class were dual door and as per TBS1 only seated 27 passengers. After rebuilding and increased seating they were never to prove popular thus these were difficult to photograph. TBS8 (FYS 772) is seen in July 1963 at Paisley Road Toll on the 108 route was quite a treat for the photographer for the only other place to capture them was usually in Hampden Park Depot! The claim to fame for the route 108 was the fact it was the last tram to trolleybus route in Great Britain. (*John Bishop*)

In 1958 Glasgow took delivery of ten 35-foot-long BUT RETB1s: they had Burlingham bodies with fifty seats and were used for the 108 route tram replacement. The depicted vehicle is No. TBS13 (FYS 988), which had the honour of being displayed at the 1958 Commercial Motor Show, and since withdrawal has been on display at the Glasgow Museum of Transport. Most of the class lasted until cessation of trolleybus services, however some did not even last two years. (*Malcolm Keeping*)

The name Hampden Park is most probably better known for its football stadium, but literally next door was one of their four trolleybus depots. This was a large open area on a slight incline to allow gravity running, as there were no overhead wires provided other than at the perimeter and exit and entrance gates. We see No. TB111 (FYS 872) and No. TB43 (FYS 804); these Crossley-bodied BUTs have just run down by gravity and are being 'poled up' to go into service, 14 July 1964. (*Malcolm Keeping*)

St Georges Square is the scene for No. TB102 (FYS 863) on route 105 to Mount Florida; this is a short working for the 105, which normally worked through to Clarkston. The date is Saturday 27 May, 1967—the last day of trolleybuses in Glasgow. The vehicle is one of a large fleet of Crossley-bodied BUT 9613Ts and is seen still in the original livery, even though many were repainted in the new, simplified livery. Also taking centre stage is the classic Ford motor home. (*John Bishop*)

Huddersfield Corporation Transport

After hostilities had ended and production resumed some semblance of normality, Huddersfield Corporation went back to Karrier with the MS2 chassis and Park Royal with the familiar pre-war three-section upper-deck window arrangement seen on No. 549 (DVH 49). There were three batches, of which No. 549 came from the second. In 1960 a number of these, No. 549 among them, were extensively rebuilt by the corporation in its workshops. The three-piece destination screen was simplified to bring these trolleys in line with the rest of the fleet. No. 549 was finally withdrawn in 1965. (*John Bishop*)

11 April 1966, a dull wet day in Newsome Road. Church spires and factory chimneys form the backdrop for this view of Roe-bodied Sunbeam MS2 No. 605 (FCX 805), delivered in 1952. One can see from this view that we are some considerable distance from the town: trolleybus routes did actually go to open country. In some instances the routes actually went beyond the borough boundary—these were the first to be withdrawn between 1961 and January 1963. (*Malcolm Keeping*)

We are near the terminus of the Longwood route, which was far from the town centre and commanded a brilliant view over the valley. Seen on 2 June 1963 is BUT 9641T with East Lancs. body No. 613 (GVH 813). This and the next batch of BUTs represented a departure from the normal specification in the use of two different manufacturers for chassis and body. The vehicle had just turned further up the road on reverser wiring on a turntable platform, constructed on concrete legs many feet above the valley. (*John Bishop*)

This could be entitled, 'A Huddersfield trolleybus seen from a most unusual angle!' The turntable referred to in the last photograph was built in 1939 due to the fact there were no other suitable locations to turn in the existing roadway. The turntable mechanism was de-activated in 1941 due to operational reasons associated with blackout regulations, and was never re-instated after the war. The overhead lines were replaced by a simple reverse triangle, a procedure which all vehicles executed until the abandonment of this route in July 1967. Our photograph was taken on 16 July 1964 showing not only the Sunbeam MS2 No. 598 (FCX 298), but the structure itself. (*Malcolm Keeping*)

The sun is setting on this smart system with a view of No. 639 (PVH 939). This was the penultimate vehicle from the last batch of ten East-Lancs.-bodied Sunbeam S7As delivered in 1959, seen turning left off the Wakefield Road on the single clockwise wiring at Waterloo on 14 March 1968. The system closed on 13 July. Note the County Motors Garage in the background. (*Malcolm Keeping*)

Ipswich Corporation

In 1948 Ipswich Corporation had ordered twenty-four Park-Royal-bodied trolleybuses numbered 103 to 126. They all looked identical, however the first six (103–108) would have Karrier W chassis to wartime specifications, while the Karrier examples 109–114 would be Karrier F4s, and the last twelve (115–126) would be Sunbeam F4s. In this view taken on 20 July 1963, we see Karrier No. 111 (PV 8868) at Tower Ramparts School more commonly referred to as 'Electric House', which was basically the hub of the trolleybus network of Ipswich. A number of features unique to Ipswich trolleybuses are visible: the mottled aluminium panels, square destination box, and the often unnoticed visor above the windscreen. (*Malcolm Keeping*)

On the Gainsborough Estate in Landseer Road at the terminal point of routes 6A and 6B is No. 117 (ADX 187), ready for the return journey to Electric House. It is 20 July 1963, literally weeks to withdrawal. No. 117 was one of last batch of Park Royal Sunbeam F4s delivered in 1950. On what must have been a warm summer's day—judging by the open front cab window—the conductor appears to be checking his ticket machine. Eight of this batch were sold for further service in Walsall, however this one would end its days in the scrap yard amid earlier post-war vehicles. (*Malcolm Keeping*)

Kingston upon Hull

One of the main roads into Kingston upon Hull was Beverley Road, the terminus of route 63, which would normally be operated by the newer Sunbeam Coronation MF2Bs. To see the Brush-bodied utility Sunbeam W No. 74 (GRH 294) was very unusual. It is 24 July 1962; the brilliant sunshine shows off the angular bodywork to advantage—it would nonetheless be withdrawn for scrap literally five weeks later. (*Malcolm Keeping*)

There cannot be a more progressive livery than that worn by the municipal buses of Kingston upon Hull, so much so that the vehicles simply had 'CORPORATION TRANSPORT' announced on the side between decks, as seen on No. 77 (GRH 297). The vehicle is a utility Brush-bodied Sunbeam W, caught on camera on 10 July 1963 at Cottingham Road. This was the junction of Newlands Avenue and terminus of route 62. Here the trolleybus would turn on the junction, which would be impractical today without lights controlling the manoeuvre. The line behind was purely for access to the nearby main depot at Cottingham Road. (*Malcolm Keeping*)

Seen at Chanterlands Avenue North in July 1962 is Roe-bodied Sunbeam W No. 82 (GRH 358), one of the eighteen-strong 'relaxed' utility vehicles delivered between 1945 and 1946. Seen at the terminus, it will be noted that it is in almost original condition. It would be withdrawn by September 1963. A feature of Hull trolleybuses was the limited use of advertisements displayed on these vehicles, if indeed they were displayed at all. It would be limited to one side of the main panel only, and this would be trimmed at the front in order to avoid covering up the stream lining. This practice can be seen on No. 82, and in addition there was limited rear advertising on the rear panel. (*John Bishop*)

No. 86 (HRH 86) was delivered in 1947. It was one of only six trolleybuses delivered that year and the last of the Sunbeam W wartime specification—elegant Roe bodies fitted with more powerful 95-hp motors. No. 86 is seen outside the city's registry office, *en route* for Holderness Road on route 64 on 10 July 1963—only ten weeks from its withdrawal. (*Malcolm Keeping*)

The first 8-foot-wide trolleybuses for Hull were ten Sunbeam F4s numbered 91 to 100 which entered service in June 1948. In addition they had automatic acceleration equipment. No. 100 (HRH 100) is seen in June 1962 at Holderness Road just yards away from the depot. By November 1963 all would be withdrawn. At the time the telephone system in Hull was an independent concern and this fact is emphasised by the green telephone box behind No. 100. (*Malcolm Keeping*)

The last trolleybuses to enter service in Hull were the very impressive Roe Sunbeam MF2Bs, popularly known as 'Coronations'. Fifteen were delivered between 1954 and 1955, with one prototype delivered the previous year in 1953. All sixteen were to remain in service until the system closed on 31 October 1964. No. 112 was photographed at Holderness Road in its last year of operation; it had served for just ten years but alas would have to go for scrap, for no buyers came forward. (*John Bishop*)

London Transport

For this publication it is not customary to view our subjects at museums, but this was the only way to depict the famous 'Diddler' trolleybus No. 1 (HX 2756) in colour, in one of its rare sorties into the open air. We see it travelling under the wires, reliving the last days of London's trolleybuses on 8 May 1962. Back on 23 September 1990, the East Anglia Transport Museum held a 'Farewell to the Diddler Day', which proved a prudent way of showing No. 1, dating from 1931, in all its glory. Just looking at the upper deck windows one can see the UCC Feltham tram design operated by the then London United Tramways and the half cab design emulating from the then current petrol bus, which indeed was the AEC Renown chassis. The bonnet was the location of the electric motor. (*John Bishop*)

At Winchmore Hill on service 641, Leyland No. 1286 (EXV 286) has literally days to go before withdrawal in November 1961.This was stage 12, which would see the end of trolleybuses through Wood Green. The running No. 57 is clearly seen behind the driver's door, along with the Wood Green Depot code plate 'WN'. The vehicle was one of 150 vehicles delivered from Leyland in 1939. (*John Bishop*)

Looking almost rural but in fact just up the road from Wood Green Depot is AEC No. 1546 (FXH 546) on route 521, bound for Central London in November 1961. This vehicle was one of the class M1, comprising twenty-five 'unit constructions' built by Weymann between November 1939 and early 1940. (*John Bishop*)

Maidstone Corporation

In the early 1960s confidence in the trolleybus was such that Maidstone Corporation not only extended their system, but embarked on re-bodying their utility trolleybuses with handsome Roe double-deck bodies, as we can see in this nearside view of No. 56 (GKP 511) on 3 October 1965. No. 56 has just completed the turning circle around the Barming village cross and the destination blind still shows the current location at Barming Bull Inn. No. 56 lasted until the last day of operations and was the lucky one of the batch to survive into preservation. It was a regular attendee at the Black Country Museum's trolleybus gatherings in the last decade. (*Malcolm Keeping*)

In this view of Northern-Coachbuilders-bodied Sunbeam W No. 72 (HKR 11) is seen at the Fountain Inn on the Tonbridge Road, Barming. It was destined to be the last Maidstone trolleybus. Still looking very smart, this 1947-built vehicle has less than eight months before withdrawal in April 1967 when photographed on 29 August 1966. It will eventually take its place at the British Trolleybus Museum at Sandtoft. Just note the cleanliness of the offside front and rear wheels. In their twenty years' service, this batch of trolleybuses had seen six variations of liveries; arguably the last (seen here) was the best proportioned, it being finished with black lining. Note the three sets of overhead wiring, with the one on the far right for turning and laying over. (*Malcolm Keeping*)

It is often said that when Maidstone Corporation acquired their last two Weymann BUTs—No. 51 and 52 from Brighton Corporation in February 1959—they added a touch of class with their well-appointed interiors and powerful 120-hp electric motors. The photograph of No. 51 (LCD 51) was taken in Wallis Avenue on the Parkwood Estate, the last extension to the system albeit for a further section inaugurated in 1963. The date was 5 November 1963—just before the bonfires were lit and the sparks about to fly! Both of these kept the Brighton fleet numbers of 51 and 52. No. 51 was the first withdrawn in 1966; No. 52 lasted until the end and was purchased for preservation at the East Anglia Transport Museum, where it currently operates still in Maidstone Corporation livery. (*Malcolm Keeping*)

Five Weymann-bodied Sunbeam Ws were acquired from Hastings upon closure of their system on 31 May 1959. They would be the last second-hand acquisitions following Llanelly and Brighton. On 5 November 1963 we see pristine No. 86 (BDY 809 and ex-34 in Hastings), having just entered Parkwood Estate from Northumberland Avenue. This vehicle and the rest from Hastings received new front panels with sealed beam head lamps when in service with Maidstone. Happily, this vehicle was also saved for preservation. (*Malcolm Keeping*)

Manchester Corporation

The distinctive Crossley 'Empire' No. 1225 (JVU 732), dating from 1949–50. It is seen to its full advantage; the rear windows on both decks are 'stepped up'. This and the sad design of the front windows made the Crossley instantly recognisable. No. 1254 is seen in June 1962 on route 210 at Hyde Gee Cross, this most unusual of terminuses, whereby the vehicle would lay over on the corner of the junction. (*Malcolm Keeping*)

The six-wheel version of the Crossley was called the 'Dominion'; it was similar to its two-axle cousin in respect of rear windows and the windscreen, and this gave the model a heavy masterful look. In this case No. 1254 (JVU 759) is just emerging from Hyde Road Depot to take up rush hour duties. It would be one of a number of trolleybuses taking up duty; a member of staff would even wear a white coat and make sure they left safely. He can just be made out at the front nearside in this photograph, taken on 8 July 1963—literally a few days before this particular vehicle was withdrawn. Another trolleybus can just be seen following No. 1254, showing the high volume of vehicles leaving Hyde Road Garage. (*Malcolm Keeping*)

Between 1955 and 1956, sixty-two Burlingham-bodied BUT 9612Ts were delivered, including No. 1337 (ONE 737), here seen in Manchester Road, Audenshaw, on 21 June 1962. It is in the original livery, complete with rear wheel trims which enhanced the vehicle. Soon afterwards this vehicle would be repainted in the all-red livery broken by a white band, however this did not save it from being withdrawn in December 1964. This location is for short working of the 218 route, which normally operates further on to Stalybridge, a further 2½ miles down the road. (*Malcolm Keeping*)

The location of this photograph is Ashton Market in July 1964. Manchester Burlingham-bodied BUT No. 1320 (ONE 720) is bathing in the morning sunshine. This shows the last variant of Manchester's almost all-red livery broken by the white band. The conductor and driver are discussing matters before setting off for Piccadilly, Manchester. Behind is an Ashton-under-Lyne Crossley 'Empire', and further back an Ashton-under-Lyne Roe-bodied Leyland PD2 Titan. (*John Bishop*)

Newcastle Corporation

March in early 1949 saw the entry into service of 36 MCCW-bodied Sunbeam F4s, numbered 443 to 478 (LBB 43 to 78), which looked slightly odd, inasmuch as they were 8 feet wide. No. 444 (LBB 44) is seen in June 1962 at the revised terminus of Denton Road and Wickham View, where a small proportion of land had been made over to facilitate the turning of the trolleybus. These would be the only 8-feet-wide, two-axle trolleybuses in the fleet, withdrawn over the period of 1961 to 1963. Note how the advertisement utilises the base yellow paintwork. (*Malcolm Keeping*)

Against a backdrop of dockyard cranes, this shot of No. 483 (LTN 483) was taken on 15 June 1964 in Welbeck Road. A BUT 9641, it went into service in April 1948 and had a MCCW body. After seventeen years No. 483 was withdrawn in May 1965. This batch of vehicles was to full London Transport specification (for instance, the destination screens) and would be known as London class Q1s. The 35 route would succumb to the diesel bus in 1965. (*Malcolm Keeping*)

Seen in central Newcastle against a very black and grimy Central Station in July 1962 is an offside view of BUT No. 498 (LTN 498), with a Q1 MCCW body. In this instance one can appreciate just how this yellow livery brightened up the streets of the area. Note the new Leyland Atlantean and, better still, the Northern-Coachbuilders-bodied AEC Regent III behind. (*John Bishop*)

We are in the west of the city, where demolition is being carried out in the summer of 1963. This is No. 516 (LTN 516), a Northern-Coachbuilders-bodied Sunbeam S7 seen on the 35 group of services at Westbourne Avenue area. This is one of thirty vehicles delivered between 1948 and 1949: this nearside view shows the precise livery description of dark red/ochre of the wings, wheels, and lining, and gleaming yellow in the bright sunshine. (*John Bishop*)

No. 539 (LTN 539) is a Sunbeam F4 with a body locally built by Northern Coachbuilders, 7 feet 6 inches wide and dating from 1950. This was one of twenty-five delivered and would see sixteen years' service. This view was taken on 9 July 1963 and has been included to show it reversing out of Byker Depot into Shields Road. Given the passing traffic and undoubtedly complicated overhead, this manoeuvre will have been executed with extreme caution—a Health and Safety nightmare today. (*Malcolm Keeping*)

Our next view is Northern-Coachbuilders-bodied 7-foot-6-inch wide BUT 9611T chassis, opposite the Central Station in July 1962. This was one from a batch of twenty-five vehicles delivered in mid-1949 and externally looked just like its Sunbeam cousins, with the same bodywork. This particular vehicle is No. 567 (LTN 567). All had gone within two years, in 1964. Even though it is mid-day, the lack of traffic is amazing in contrast to road conditions today. The wings at the back and front were painted black, but in fact they were made of rubber, a common feature of public transport of that period. (*John Bishop*)

We have an obvious bias in favour of this marque of trolleybus—don't they look grand? With the first and last batches of MCCW of Q1 type BUT 9641Ts, one can compare and see the differences in the designs of No. 604 (NBB 604), and behind it No. 498 (LTN 498). The later batch numbers, 579–628, were to Newcastle's specifications: their standard destination display was the most obvious, but also the interior fitments and sliding windows. They would remain in service until the last day of operations on 1 October 1966 and are seen here in Osborne Road in July 1964. (*Malcolm Keeping*)

Nottingham Corporation

The war years stretched the ageing pre-war fleet so the Nottingham Corporation took delivery of utility specification trolleybuses, numbered 442 to 478. The fifth batch of utility vehicles were Roe-bodied Karriers numbered 459 to 465 and dating from 1945. These had the associated utility angular design, but still had the trademark of Roe products—the thick beading below the lower window from the driver's cab round to the rear. Note it here on No. 461 (GTV 661) at Wilford Road in August 1962. (*John Bishop*)

In this view we see No. 475 (HAU 175) from the last batch delivered in early 1946 but still very much to wartime specifications. This Park-Royal-bodied Karrier W enjoys the summer sun in August 1962, waiting at Wells Road for the departure across the city to Wilford Road. Note the clock on the traction pole—very much a feature of the system. Despite receiving a thorough overhaul in 1959 (after sixteen years' service), No. 475 was withdrawn and sold for scrap in May 1963. (*John Bishop*)

In 1948 Nottingham Corporation purchased two small batches of two-axle trolleybuses, numbered 479 to 495. The first four were Roe-bodied Karrier Ws and the rest were Roe-bodied BUT 9611Ts. In this photograph taken on 25 June 1962 at Wilford Road, we see Karrier W No. 480 (KTV 480) having just emptied the passengers before moving off round a roundabout to our right. Note the distinctive red colour of the wheels which contrasts with the green livery. (*Malcolm Keeping*)

The second batch of two-axle vehicles delivered in 1948 represented here by Roe-bodied BUT 9611T No. 495, (KTV 495), in Wilford Road. This was the usual haunt for the two-axle vehicles, although after withdrawal the three-axle BUTs would cope admirably. Pictured in August 1962, No. 495 (last of the batch) looks pristine. Notice the differences in the two batches, with the screen here being slightly deeper and the shifting location of the front lights. No. 495 was withdrawn and sold for scrap in May 1965. (*John Bishop*)

Between 1948 and 1952, just over 100 Brush-bodied BUT 9641Ts were delivered. Here we see No. 508 (KTV 508) on route 39, Middleton Boulevard at Wollaton Park. This was the terminus of routes 39 and 45, but by the time this photograph was taken in June 1965, route 45 had already been replaced by motorbuses back in November 1962. Route 39 would suffer the same fate in September 1965, some twelve weeks hence. It is appropriate to point out at this stage that the first deliveries (numbered 500 to 524) were 8 feet wide, while subsequent deliveries (525 to 601) were 7 feet 6 inches wide. [See the final two photographs in this section] (*Malcolm Keeping*)

A bustling scene in the city centre—trolleybuses galore! No. 536 (KTV 536), a BUT 9641T with a 7-foot-6-inch-wide Brush body in August 1963, just before withdrawal the following month. To our right is the market square and council office. Today this part of town is traversed by the Nottingham tram system, which turns to our right. Note the Triumph Herald Coupe, Morris Minor 1000, and Minivan—all made in Great Britain. As for trolleybus No. 536, its fate was sealed in April 1964, when it was sold for scrap. (*John Bishop*)

Above and below: Observe the difference between the 8-feet wide body of No. 503 and 7-foot-6-inch wide body of No. 582, taken at the same location on 26 April 1964. No. 503 is equipped to remind the driver of its width by virtue of its white steering wheel, whereas No. 582 has a black steering wheel. (*Malcolm Keeping*)

Portsmouth

The focal point of the Portsmouth system was the dockyard gates, where we see Craven-bodied AEC No. 250 (RV 8332) and No. 248 (RV 8330), only yards away from HMS *Victory* in 1962. These two veterans of the fleet look in fine condition after twenty seven years' service. These two trolleybuses both travelled from Eastney to the Dockyard on route 17, and then returned on route 18. As you can see, vehicles appeared to park wherever they liked, but there was a system whereby the three trolley wire lines all converged into one; they would then turn behind the photographer, by the dock gates in the road, and head in the opposite way towards the city, past the buses on the right. (*Malcolm Keeping*)

Portsmouth was still having a love affair with the trolleybus right up until 1951, when route 15/16 from Floating Bridge to Copnor via the High Street was withdrawn, coinciding with the delivery of the last fifteen Burlingham-bodied BUT 9611Ts, Nos. 301 to 315. No. 314 (ERV 939) is seen in 1962 at Eastney on route 6, inbound from Cosham. The choice of the Burlingham was unusual, inasmuch as HV Burlingham were more associated with coach bodies; nevertheless, it cannot be denied that they offered handsome lines. Another unusual feature was the offside ultimate destination screen. Note the deserted road—such an opportunity for a photographer would virtually never present itself today. Thankfully, sister vehicle No. 313 (ERV 938) has been fully restored and can be seen recalling the golden years of Portsmouth trolleybuses at the East Anglia Transport Museum. (*Malcolm Keeping*)

Reading Corporation

Park-Royal-bodied BUT 9611T speeds along Oxford Road, as indicated by the early road sign on the traction pole. Entering service in 1949, No.149 was withdrawn in January 1967 just short of eighteen years' service. Sister vehicle No. 144 was used for the official last trolleybus operation when the system closed on 3 November 1968. Today the sisters are regular performers at the Trolleybus Museum in Sandtoft. (*Malcolm Keeping*)

Caught by the camera one sunny Sunday in 1962: Park-Royal-bodied Sunbeam S7 No. 180 (ERD 151) in the town centre. St Mary's Butts can just be seen on the right, a scene which has changed little since this was taken, save for the traffic management schemes now blighting many of our towns. Until 1964 route numbers were not incorporated, however the white backing was removed to facilitate the triple route number box when the routes were numbered. Compared with the 120-hp electric motors in the two-axle BUTs, these Sunbeams with their 95-hp motors and 10-ton weight must have proved comparatively sluggish. No. 180 was withdrawn in January 1968 and all the class was gone by November that year. Fortunately Nos. 174 and 181 have been preserved. (*Malcolm Keeping*)

No. 190 (VRD 190) in 1962, having completed one year of its short working life in Reading. Still looking new, it was one of twelve Burlingham-bodied Sunbeam F4As numbered from 182 to 193 with corresponding registrations (VRD 182 to 193). No. 190 was one of the unlucky ones, withdrawn in November 1968 and sent for scrap in April 1969. This batch suffered with ventilation problems and had to have louvers fitted to the offside of the body and extra opening windows. Here the No. 190 is still so new that it has not yet had any modifications. (*Malcolm Keeping*)

The Sunbeam F4As delivered in 1961 would only enjoy a comparatively short life, being withdrawn in 1968. Seen in Norcot on its way to Tilehurst on 28 July 1968 is No. 186 (VRD 186), with but another four months before being withdrawn on 2 November, one day before final closure. Five of the class were sold to the Teeside Railless Traction Board. No. 186 was one of the lucky ones, though: it became No. 11 in April 1969 in their small fleet, and was later renumbered T291. Ironically, it was this vehicle that became the ceremonial last trolleybus in the Teeside fleet and was ultimately preserved. In its eight short years of service, No. 186 had served two trolleybus systems, had been the last ceremonial vehicle at Teeside, and then escaped the torch. (*John Bishop*)

Construction work started in August 1967 for the new ring road which was to pass under Oxford Road. This required the road to be completely removed one half at a time. A one-way system was set up which required all traffic to be diverted, however trolleybuses were allowed to continue in view of their fixed wiring. The road was controlled by a set of traffic lights controlled by the driver himself, who pressed a button on a box by the roadside to give east-bound trolleybuses safe passage through the narrow one-way section. As the trolleybus passed through, the lights would return to their original settings, automatically allowing west-bound trolleybuses to flow through safely. Here we see Burlingham-bodied Sunbeam No. 187 (VRD 187) about to enter the 'no-go area'. Finally, note the characteristic round corners of the windows associated with Burlingham double-deckers. (*John Bishop*)

Rotherham Corporation

On a blistering hot day in June 1963, a visit to the rear of the Rotherham Corporation Depot revealed this splendid single-decker East-Lancs.-bodied Daimler type CT awaiting its fate, having been withdrawn for a while. This particular vehicle, No. 6 (FET 610) had the fleet number 10 when originally delivered in 1950. In 1960 seventeen of these vehicles were exported to Spain, where they gave over another ten years' service. Fifteen went to Cadiz where they were re-bodied, while two went to the San Sebastián/Tolosa system, where they remained in original condition. (John Bishop)

Thrybergh Terminus on route 6, 2 June 1963. No. 43 (FET 616) has just negotiated the tight turning circle according to the black wheel marks on the road surface. No. 43 started life as a single-deck Daimler numbered 16, gaining the double-deck Roe body in 1956 following an in-depth review of trolleybus operations. It was felt that the extra carrying capacity would make trolleybus operations more remunerative. (*John Bishop*)

With the road stretching out towards Doncaster we see No. 30 (FET 339) and previously No. 79), inbound to Rotherham on route 6 from Thrybergh. This vehicle once again was re-bodied by Roe in 1956 along with nineteen others. The small road sign states Doncaster is 10 miles away, itself an operator of trolleybuses. Interestingly, moves were afoot in 1928, with a proposal for the operation of a trolleybus route via Conisbrough to Doncaster, but this never materialised. After fifty-three years of operation, the system finally closed on 2 October 1965. (*Malcolm Keeping*)

South Shields Corporation

The market was the hub of the South Shields system, and here we can see three trolleybuses, headed by No. 212 (CU 3854) from the third batch of Weymann-bodied Karrier E4s (Nos. 208 to 233) in July 1962. The system at its zenith would be a hive of activity, so much so that waiting vehicles would frequently have to de-pole—as they are doing here—and re-pole immediately afterwards. The Weymann bodies were of composite construction, with the centre section of the roof constructed with wooden slats covered in canvas. During their twenty-five years' service they saw little alteration to the bodywork, save for the repositioning of the side lights and an extra route number box. By April 1963 No. 212 was no more, having been scrapped. Note the bent trolley on the Northern-Coachbuilders-bodied Sunbeam No. 261 (CU 5100), and how the trolleybus stops make up for the information not seen on the trolleybus destination screen! (*John Bishop*)

At the Marsden Inn on a sunny day in July 1962, we see 'relaxed' utility specification Roe-bodied Karrier W No. 249 (CU 4719), delivered in January 1947. The body was little altered except for the fitment of a route number box, and No. 249 retired in March 1963 after sixteen years. A feature of South Shields was the fitment of brackets just above the lower deck window, on the nearside of the vehicle for the bamboo retrieving pole, rather than the usual location under the vehicle at the rear. (*John Bishop*)

In this view we can again see clearly the bamboo pole on the nearside of Northern-Coachbuilders-bodied Karrier W4 No. 251 (CU 4873). This is numerically the first of the batch of twenty Northern-Coachbuilder-bodied examples delivered between 1947 and 1950. Numerically, this is the first of the batch of twenty Northern-Coachbuilder-bodied examples delivered between 1947 and 1948. It could be easily distinguished from the batch delivered in 1950 by the same body manufacturer by the extra waist rail beading below each deck of windows (see the following photograph). As No. 251 slows to make the left turn the phrase 'hop on, hop off' comes to mind, as a gentleman jumps off the rear platform! (*John Bishop*)

This photograph speaks volumes—old traffic signs, policemen on the beat, and replacement, modernist architecture as a result of the heavy air raids sustained in the market area. The date is June 1962. We see ex St Helens East-Lancs.-bodied Sunbeam F4 turning off the market on route 12 for Marsden Inn. This vehicle, No. 206 (BDJ 78), started life as St Helens as No. 178 and entered service at South Shields after overhaul in January 1959. It remained in service for only four years, withdrawn in April 1963. These eight vehicles were the only 8-foot-wide trolleybuses to operate in South Shields. (*Malcolm Keeping*)

We are at the market for this offside view of No. 265 (CU 5104), looking absolutely pristine in the summer sun of July 1963. No. 265 represents the final batch of new vehicles delivered in 1950 and shows the cleaner appearance of the Northern Coachbuilders bodywork, with one line of beading below each window. These also had 'push-out vents' on the front upper windows. By the time of the delivery of this batch of Sunbeam F4s, the name Karrier had gone (1948), but the department would still refer to these as Karriers. (*John Bishop*)

In 1957 South Shields turned to the second-hand market to replace some of their ageing earlier vehicles, and thereby acquired four Park-Royal-bodied Karrier W4 utility trolleybuses to relaxed specifications from Pontypridd in 1957. Delivered in 1946, they were de-licensed in 1956 and re-entered service with South Shields in 1957, with only the destination boxes being rebuilt. Here, in July 1962, we see No. 238 (FTG 234 and ex-12 at Pontypridd) at Tyne Dock. The rubber-mounted destination screens are clearly visible. (*John Bishop*)

Teeside Railless Traction Board/
Teeside Municipal Transport

On 15 June 1964 at North Ormesby we see No. 10 (CPY 308), now with a new Roe body on the Sunbeam W chassis—a testament of the Teeside Railless Traction Board's faith in the trolleybus. All the utility-bodied Sunbeams were treated between 1960 and '62 except for No. 11 which went for scrap. While the traffic conditions look light, the practical reality is that turning trolleybuses on this junction very often proved horrendous; thus the traffic lights which control this 'T' junction were controlled by a trip switch on the overhead. The trolleybus activated the lights, which turned to red, and the driver would negotiate the tight turn uninterrupted. The road to the left behind us would take you into Middlesbrough. Note the school in the background and the advance school sign before the advent of continental road signs. (*Malcolm Keeping*)

The concept of a temporary diversion for a trolleybus route was virtually unheard of in the UK. However, in the last five years of trolleybus operation in Teeside, just that happened. For a period of eight months between March and October 1966 the main Middlesbrough road and the bridge close to the Cargo Fleet Depot was closed to through traffic. This eight-month closure was necessary to completely rebuild the railway bridge and make good the approach roads, and meant that the trolleybus service was severed in two. To overcome this problem, the unprecedented step was taken to erect temporary overhead wiring along the old Middlesbrough road, which was a side road incorporating a rail level crossing. Here is No. 17 (CPY 288), a Roe re-bodied Sunbeam W negotiating the temporary wiring over the railway line. The short diversion consisted of traction poles with bracket arms except at the crossing depicted, where the overhead is supported by span wires stretching for a considerable distance. The date of this unique photograph was 28 August 1966. (*Malcolm Keeping*)

There is so much to see outside Cargo Fleet Depot. On our left, a rear view of Roe re-bodied Sunbeam W No. 13 (CPY 311), on 28 August 1966. Long before its time, a road safety triangle was built into the body, and when the vehicle made its turn the whole section would illuminate. Under normal circumstances the line went to our left over a railway bridge, however due to protracted road works to rebuild the bridge the road and trolleybus overhead was diverted right on a temporary basis over a level crossing, where we can see No. 15 (CPY 286) emerging. (*Malcolm Keeping*)

In 1950 Teeside took delivery of seven well-proportioned East-Lancs.-bodied Sunbeam F4s, like No. 6 here at the Kingsley Road Terminus in July 1962. At this stage the system was still at its original length. The gentleman and the children, all neatly aligned from eldest to toddler, together with the lady in the door of the house are gazing at a tame bird which has escaped and is sitting over a neighbour's house making one heck of a noise! (*John Bishop*)

Between 1962 and 1965 it was possible to see both old and new bodies side by side. The trolleybuses were given new Roe bodies, as can be seen in this instance at Normanby. At the front is Roe-bodied Sunbeam W No. 16 (CPY 287). No. 4 (GAJ 14), a Sunbeam F4 with its original East Lancs. bodywork, overtakes after the driver has de-poled the trolleys, while the conductor looks on. Note that the nearside door is open on the front vehicle for access into the driver's cab. (*John Bishop*)

April 1968 saw the formation of Teeside Municipal Transport upon the merging of the three municipal transport undertakings: Middlesbrough, Stockton, and of course the Teeside Railless Traction Board. The adopted livery of turquoise and two white bands with black wings and wheels can be observed on No. 13 (CPY 311), one of the Roe re-bodied Sunbeam Ws at North Ormesby. (*John Bishop*)

As a follow on from the previous photograph of No. 13, we see a nearside view of Roe re-bodied Sunbeam F4 No. 2 (GAJ 12). It is wearing the final version of the Teeside Municipal livery—one white band picked out with black lines—and branded 'TEESIDE MUNICIPAL TRANSPORT'. (*Malcolm Keeping*)

In the final purchase of trolleybuses in 1969, five forward entrance Burlingham-bodied Sunbeam F4As arrived from Reading after that system closed. These had been new to Reading in 1961. These and the older re-bodied Sunbeam Ws and F4s kept the system going until the end, which came on 4 April 1971. The fleet number for this vehicle is No. 12 (VRD 192). It is seen going through Eston Market towards Normanby on the new extension, inaugurated on 31 March 1968—the last extension constructed in the UK. (*Malcolm Keeping*)

Walsall Corporation

In this July 1963 scene we see No. 333 (JDH 434) on learner duties with Sunbeam F4A No. 861 (behind). The road in the background leads down to the bus station. No. 333 is a 1946 Sunbeam W with Roe bodywork which has had an amount of rebuilding done on the front: it has been given a rounded destination aperture and has been rubber-mounted, as have the upper deck windows. It would be another two years before this vehicle would be withdrawn in 1965. (*John Bishop*)

We are at Blakenall for this view of No. 339 (NDH 956) at the turning circle, where she is receiving some attention by the depot crew. The date is June 1962. This Brush-bodied Sunbeam F4 dating from 1950 would soldier on until 1970, when the last of the class were withdrawn. This is a credit not only to the manufacturers, but to the staff at the corporation workshops. Note how the beading has been picked out in dark blue. (*Malcolm Keeping*)

A sunny day in July 1963. An offside shot of No. 336 (NDH 953), waiting for the road to clear. The Brush-bodied Sunbeam F4 shows a variant of the livery, with dark blue lines on the beading and a wide dark blue line below the lower deck windows. (*John Bishop*)

A scene at the central bus station on 19 September 1968 with a very much rebuilt Brush-bodied Sunbeam F4 No. 342 (NDH 959). The vehicle dates from 1951 and was lengthened at the corporation workshops. One can see the extra window bay behind the driver's cab and the remounting of the windows with white rubber. The chassis should arguably be classified as a Sunbeam F4A rather than a F4. Note the de-poled Willowbrook-bodied Sunbeam F4A and ex-Ipswich Sunbeam waiting to depart. (*Malcolm Keeping*)

In 1953, Walsall Corporation took delivery of No. 350 (RDH 990), which was used for a 'Pay as you Enter' experiment and like other similar schemes elsewhere was not deemed a success. The Willowbrook body was mounted on a Sunbeam S7 chassis and rebuilt back to the normal configuration. The vehicle was originally fleet number 850 but was renumbered to 350 in 1961. Here No. 350 is seen at Blakenall. She was finally withdrawn in May 1967. (*Malcolm Keeping*)

In 1954 and 1956 twenty-two new 30-foot-long Sunbeam F4As with Willowbrook bodies were purchased following special dispensation from the Ministry of Transport, for they were only on two axles. This was a first in Britain. Another factor with the Willowbrook body was the weight, reduced to 7¼ tons—an important factor in the consumption of electricity. Here No. 854 (TDH 904) speeds back to the town centre along the Lower Farm Estate in September 1968. (*Malcolm Keeping*)

With impending cost-cutting in mind, General Manager Edgeley Cox had one of the Sunbeam F4As, No. 866 (XDH 66), converted from rear entrance to forward entrance. The conversion did nothing to stem the flow of closure, especially after the acquisition upon the formation of the West Midlands Passenger Transport Executive. We can see No. 866's town crests have been removed and new legal lettering applied as it speeds towards Blakenall in September 1970, only four weeks before the final closure. (*Malcolm Keeping*)

The year 1959 saw the arrival of eight Weymann-bodied Sunbeam Ws from Hastings upon closure of the system there. These were numbered 303 to 310 and must have been a durable acquisition, lasting until 1970. Walsall carried out a number of alterations; the most noticeable were the remounting of the windows and destination boxes with white moulding rubbers. They made other changes to their details, including sealed beam headlights—although the Sunbeam W caught here, No. 303 (BDY 806), still had its original headlights. On 16 July 1963 we see No. 303 at St James's Square, Wolverhampton, on the joint route from Walsall to Wolverhampton. (*Malcolm Keeping*)

Two interesting vehicles arrived from Grimsby-Cleethorpes in 1961: two Roe-bodied Crossley Empires. Their distinctive style stood out from the rest of the fleet, like that of No. 873 (HBE 542), seen in the Dudley Fields Estate in July 1964. No. 873 was to remain in the fleet until 1967, however its partner, No. 850, soldiered on until the system's closure in October 1970. (*Malcolm Keeping*)

The second ex-Grimsby Roe-bodied Crossley Empire, No. 850 (HBE 541), standing at the bus station in Walsall. It stands quite apart in front of an ex-Hastings Weymann-bodied Sunbeam W. Further back, one of the Willowbrook Sunbeam F4As. (*John Bishop*)

In 1962 Walsall Corporation acquired four ex-Grimsby-Cleethorpes BUT 9611Ts with Northern Coachbuilder bodies. Three of the class were rebuilt with a front entrance and lengthened to 30 feet, drastically altering their appearance. Yet they still kept their neat outline, like No. 877 (GFU 695) here, on 3 June 1963 on the Beechdale Estate soon after its conversion. In the background is one of the Willowbrook-bodied Sunbeam F4As, No. 853, trying to get into the photograph. (*Malcolm Keeping*)

One of the ex-Grimsby-Cleethorpes BUT 9611Ts *not* rebuilt: No. 874 (GFU 692) on the Moseley Estate. While this is an offside view, one can still determine the vehicle is still the original length and the staircase is at the rear. (*John Bishop*)

73

The last purchases by Walsall Corporation were eight Sunbeam F4s with Park Royal bodies. They had been part of the last batch purchased by Ipswich Corporation. Here we see No. 353 (ADX 151), having just left the bus station in September 1968. They were famous for their mottled aluminium panels, but were soon painted into the standard livery of Walsall blue with three yellow lines. Intriguingly, they kept the Ipswich destination boxes, utilising their own version very well—'30 CIRCULAR VIA LEAMORE'. (*John Bishop*)

Wolverhampton Corporation

This Roe re-bodied Sunbeam W, No. 419 (DUK 419), is seen at Bushbury Hill Terminus in glorious sunshine in June 1963 on route 3. Its Roe body is but five years old. On its way back to the town centre, No. 419 will pass the Guy factory, where many of the town's vehicles were constructed, and the Wolverhampton Corporation Park Lane Depot. (*John Bishop*)

'Two for the price of one' at Fighting Cocks Terminus: No. 434 (EJW 434) and No. 411 (DJW 941). No. 434 is a Sunbeam W which started life with a Park Royal body; in the early 1960s, this and the rest of the batch of vehicles numbered 434 to 455 were re-bodied by Roe. Angular No. 411 was a utility and also re-bodied by Park Royal. This photograph was taken on 30 March 1964. (*John Bishop*)

Seen negotiating a roundabout is No. 468 (FJW 468), from the penultimate batch of Sunbeams with Park Royal bodywork. Dating from 1948, these were 8 feet wide and had a white steering wheel, seen clearly here in June 1963. (*Malcolm Keeping*)

Photographed in June 1963 in the town centre of Wolverhampton in one of the many side streets which trolleybuses were to be found 1948 Park-Royal-bodied Sunbeam F4 is number 471 – FJW 471. It is one of a small number of trolleybuses painted in this all over dark green livery as an experiment in 1959 which was not continued. No. 471 remained in service for a further 17 months being finally withdrawn in November 1964. (*Malcolm Keeping*)

In this 1963 view in the town centre it is a job to concentrate on the view of number 482 (FJW 482), a 1949 Park-Royal-bodied Guy BT with all the various advertisements of the time. These looked virtually the same as the previous deliveries of Sunbeam trolleybuses in 1948 (fleet numbers 456 to 481), however, to the discerning, the rear axle was more pointed. Here we can see No. 482 is just about to pull away, by virtue of the small hand protruding out of the driver's window of the door! (*John Bishop*)

2

Driving School Vehicles

Like in all fields of transport, there was always a need for driver training vehicles, and very often it was the oldest vehicles in the fleet which were used for this purpose. Nottingham Corporation No. 463 (GTV 683), a wartime utility Karrier W with Roe bodywork, is seen in Nottingham Road at the Hayden Road turning circle of route 37. The trainee driver is evidently getting tips from the instructor sitting in the cab with the driver. This photograph was taken on 25 June 1962, just five months before this vehicle's withdrawal. (*Malcolm Keeping*)

The general rule was that the older vehicle is used for driver training, but sometimes the unexpected happened, as in this view of Walsall Corporation No. 342 (NDH 959). As explained earlier in the Walsall Corporation section, this vehicle was drastically rebuilt to extend the chassis, and was therefore a useful asset for familiarising students with the 30-foot chassis. No. 342 was photographed in the bus station on 19 September 1968—interesting that just two years away from closure, new drivers were still in demand. For the uninitiated there was (and still) is a separate category to drive a trolley vehicle, though the future for the trolleybus was very much bleak. (*Malcolm Keeping*)

Bradford Corporation had a number of training vehicles, all numbered in their own series. No. 060 was a Roe-bodied BUT, and one of the first batch of ten vehicles delivered to Bradford in 1949, when it was given fleet number 745. In February 1964 it was withdrawn from passenger service and later in June of that year joined the training school. After four years it was returned to service and finally withdrawn in January 1972. This view of No. 060 was taken at Saltaire on training duties on 21 July 1964. Note the instructor sat at the front again and a dedicated board affixed to the front of the vehicle. (*Malcolm Keeping*)

Manchester Corporation all-Crossley Empire No. 1237 (JVU 744) was one of thirty-eight similar vehicles delivered in October 1949 and is seen here with the 'L' plate clipped on the front. The outward condition of No. 1237 when photographed here on 8 July 1963 at the loop in Audenshaw indicates that it is near the end of its life—indeed it was withdrawn just days afterwards. The turning loop was used for the short workings for routes 215 and 218X. (*Malcolm Keeping*)

Seen at Walsall is No. 850 (HBE 541), ex-Grimsby-Cleethorpes Roe-bodied Crossley Empire on learner duties and still looking smart late in life. In comparison to some of our earlier views, it will be noted, the modern 'Give Way' sign has been installed at the road junction in place of the 'Slow Major Road' sign. (*John Bishop*)

Blank screens; learner plate; impending dark skies. Roe-bodied Sunbeam W No. 411 (DUK 831) pulls out to the centre of the road to turn left into Court Road. Devotees of the British Motor Corporation will appreciate the sparkling Austin A60 parked at the front of the public house, the Austin A40 Farina, and the red Mini. (*John Bishop*)

3

Joint Trolleybus Operations

Joint operations were on three routes for Manchester and Ashton-under-Lyne Corporations: 217, 218, and 219, which radiated out of Ashton-under-Lyne. They went to Stalybridge, Haughton Green, and to west, central Manchester. Introduced in 1938 and 1940, the 217 was converted to bus operation in 1960, followed by the 219 in October 1964, and finally the 218 in December 1966. This view taken on 13 July 1964 shows Ashton-under-Lyne all-Crossley vehicle No. 80 passing Manchester No. 1341, a 1955 Burlingham-bodied BUT laying over at Audenshaw on the inside lane. (*Malcolm Keeping*)

Wolverhampton and Walsall jointly operated service 29, inaugurated on 16 November 1931. It operated between the two towns for thirty-four years, until 31 October 1965. 8th July 1965, St James Square: Wolverhampton Roe-bodied Sunbeam W No. 451 (EJW 451) is on route 5 to Willenhall, which was basically a short working of the route 29. The rear vehicle is an ex-Ipswich Park-Royal-bodied Sunbeam F4 No. 345 (ADX 194). These vehicles were a familiar sight on route 29 in the last few months of joint operation. The cooling towers in the background make for an unglamorous backdrop! (*Malcolm Keeping*)

4

Depot Views

South Shields had two depots which were built back to back for the tram fleet. The first was built in 1906 to the traditional layout, with the lower depot added in 1925 for the expanding fleet. The tram replacement programme commenced in 1938 with trolleybuses, and the last tram bowed out on 31 March, 1946. This was taken in the first depot on 9 July 1963, showing the tram lines still in place. The two vehicles depicted are No. 256 (CU 4943), a Karrier W4 of 1947, and on the left a 1950 Sunbeam F4, No. 264 (CU 5103). Both have bodywork by Northern Coachbuilders. (*Malcolm Keeping*)

Southcote Road, Bournemouth, would be the main depot for Bournemouth Corporation trolleybuses, having housed the tram fleet before them. We can see the tram origins as the vehicles straddle the pits, for instance No. 219 (BEL 814), a 1935 Park Royal Sunbeam MS2. Note the ex-Brighton BUT alongside it. Believe it or not, the sun was shining very brightly outside! (*John Bishop*)

Brighton Corporation trolleybuses were all housed at the Lewes Road Depot in Brighton. No. 38 (FUF 38) heads a line-up of Weymann-bodied AECs and again there is no hiding the tramway origins, although the flooring has already been filled and a smooth concrete floor laid. To the left is one of the replacement buses from stage one. (*John Bishop*)

Longroyd Bridge Depot is the setting for this view of Huddersfield East-Lancs.-bodied BUT No. 607 (GVH 807). No. 607 is standing between two iron structures used for the servicing of the trolleybuses. This depot was originally built for the trams and rebuilt in the late 1930s for the new trolleybus fleet, as seen in this view on 11 October 1964. Note the line of Daimler and Leyland diesel buses on the left-hand side; they were used for the trolleybus replacement conversion programme. (*Malcolm Keeping*)

Our last depot view is in Newcastle. Trolleybuses in general tended to inherit old tram depots with cobbled entrances and the remains of tram lines. Some fleets had purpose-built buildings and one such fleet was in Newcastle. During the trolleybus era four depots had been used; one in particular, Wingrove Road, was to house the initial 1935 fleet. In 1956 this was replaced by a purpose-built depot at Fenham, known as Slatyford Depot. Seen on 9 July 1963 is trolleybus No. 512 (LTN 512), a Northern-Coachbuilders-bodied Sunbeam S7 dating from 1949 standing on the forecourt with the poles down and the depot façade as the backdrop. This building also housed motorbuses and the substation for the overhead lines. (*Malcolm Keeping*)

5

Preserved Trolleybuses
on Tour

As the final curtain started to descend on trolleybuses, so those already in preservation operated on the remaining systems. One such system was Reading, where we see open-top Bournemouth Corporation Sunbeam MS2, 202 with Park Royal bodywork by the depot in Mill Lane. Parked on a Sunday is a line-up of Burlingham-bodied Sunbeam F4As. This area has completely changed with closure of the garage and construction of 'The Oracle' shopping complex. (*John Bishop*)

The opening of the last trolleybus extension in Britain took place in Teeside on 31 March 1968. This was only hours before the merger of the Teeside Railless Traction Board with Middlesbrough Corporation and Stockton Corporation, which created a new and much larger transport undertaking, the 'Teeside Municipal Transport'. After this took effect on 1 April 1968, a new livery of turquoise was adopted for the three operators. To mark the opening of the new extension, preserved trolleybus No. 6340 (CPM 61), a 1939 Weymann-bodied AEC from the Brighton Hove & District fleet, was towed from its temporary home at Charing, Kent, to the Cargo Fleet Depot of Teeside Railless Traction Board, where it was checked over and was pronounced fit for service. Not bad for a vehicle which had not been used for over nine years! On Sunday 31 March, No. 6340 followed the official trolleybus No. 3 around the new overhead wiring for the first time, linking the Normanby route with Grangetown route. A second tour was arranged for the benefit of a number of enthusiasts on 5 May 1968, and No. 6340 once again made an appearance. This view shows it in the very small depot at Cargo Fleet in the company of two of the residents— No. 6 Sunbeam F4 and No. 10 Sunbeam W, both of which were re-bodied by Roe in the 1960s. (*Malcolm Keeping*)

6

The Final Chapter

The words say it all: 'Britain's Last Trolleybus 1911–1972'. The last British trolleybus ran in Bradford on the afternoon of 26 March 1972; here, Sunbeam No. 844 (FWX 914) stands shining in the sun on the private road leading to the car works adjacent to Thornbury Depot. It will shortly travel down Leeds Road accompanied by the Austin tower wagon No. 032 seen behind to the impressive Bradford city hall, where a crowd has gathered outside the main entrance. (*Malcolm Keeping*)

No. 844 is parked outside the city hall with the police on duty; a path has been kept clear for the Lord Mayor to emerge from his chambers at 3.00 p.m., wearing his ceremonial chain of office. He will walk down the steps onto No. 844. This was taken literally seconds before he descended the steps and the vehicle departed for the rest of the guests at Thornton Road. The party would then depart for the very last trolleybus journey on public roads in Britain to Thornton. (*Malcolm Keeping*)

It was not until 4.30 p.m. that No. 844 returned back to Thornbury Depot to hundreds of onlookers, all waiting to see the last few minutes of trolleybus operation in Britain. Buses and cars were brought to a standstill in Leeds Road and the police had to step in to control the situation, but not until all the photographs had been taken! The clouds are were gathering and the curtain finally falling as No. 844 arrived back for the very last time. (*Malcolm Keeping*)

7

Rest in Peace

No one wishes to see trolleybuses in scrap yards, least of all a London vehicle. After all, London was once the showpiece system. Whereas post-war BUTs went to Spain, the pre-war vehicles went to Cohen's, situated behind Colindale Trolleybus Depot on the Edgware Road. It is November 1961, and we see Nos. 1309 and 1344 (EXV 309 and 344) almost wallowing in the mud and dirt. A sad end indeed. (*John Bishop*)

Brighton Corporation No. 1 (FUF1) in its final resting place at Light's scrap yard, Southerham, near Lewes, in the early 1960s and complete with epitaph—'1939 Brighton Trolleybuses 1961'. The vehicle was later pushed over onto its side and all the valuable electrical gear removed. No. 1 is seen complete with words. The number plate has disappeared; no doubt it now adorns some enthusiast's wall! (*John Bishop*)

'What might have been?' In June 1985 serious proposals were made for the re-introduction of trolleybuses, so an Alexander-bodied Dennis experimental vehicle was built for South Yorkshire Passenger Transport Executive. The trolleybus was given fleet number 2450 and registered as C45 HDT. An open day was set for 8 September 1985, where the vehicle was demonstrated to enthusiasts and locals alike. Regretfully the scheme came to nothing, beaten in the end by legislation, and No. 2450 was assigned to the Sandtoft Trolleybus Museum, where this photograph was taken. (*John Bishop*)

8

Trolleybus Ancillary Service Vehicles

Without service vehicles, trolleybus systems would not have survived the day's tasks—from replacement of carbon skids for the overhead current collection to de-wirement when the trolley booms came off the overhead or other associated calamities. This picture shows a Portsmouth Corporation tower lorry for the repair of the overhead wiring. This tower wagon No. TW1 (RV 3411) was converted from Leyland TD2 motor bus No. 17 in 1952, and fortunately made it to preservation. No. TW1 is visible at the rear of Eastney Depot in the access road. (*John Bishop*)

London Transport made use of purpose-built vehicles for repairs on the road, one example of which is this Leyland Cub light open-backed lorry in April 1962. It is about to leave Fulwell Depot to attend to another incident. (*John Bishop*)

Teeside Railless Traction Board in North Yorkshire acquired a number of tower wagons by hiring or purchasing from former trolleybus operators. These included a petrol-engined Bedford, acquired from Rotherham in 1965, and a second Bedford, acquired from Cardiff Corporation in 1970. A 1938 vintage Karrier from South Shields was also put to use, as well as a pre-war Leyland Lynx from West Hartlepool. Here pictured is a Thornycroft which started life with Hull Corporation in 1943 and came to Teeside in October 1967; it is towing Sunbeam No. 3 into the Cargo Fleet Depot on 3 April 1969. It was a common practice among trolleybus operators to use their tower wagons for towing duties, depot roof repairs, and general maintenance. (*Malcolm Keeping*)

Glasgow Corporation trolleybuses Nos. TB77 and TB79 are both in trouble. BUT No. TB77 had lowered its trolley booms to negotiate the road works and the driver has switched to battery, however the batteries are not fit enough and the trolleybus soon has come to a standstill. A few minutes later, No. TB79 arrives hoping to pass both No. TB77 and the hole in the road, but it too becomes stranded for exactly the same reasons! This scene was caught on camera on 1 July 1965, minutes after the maintenance team had arrived with the towing vehicle. The vehicle was one of a number of AEC Regents delivered in 1938 with Cowiesen double-deck bodies; they were subsequently re-bodied in 1950 by Scottish Commercial. In more recent times a number were converted to towing duties. (*Malcolm Keeping*)

Active Trolleybus Museums

Today one can still witness the trolleybus in action at the Sandtoft Trolleybus Museum, near Doncaster, South Yorkshire (www.sandtoft.org.uk).

East Anglia Transport Museum, Carlton Colville, near Lowestoft, Suffolk (www.eatm. org.uk).

Black Country Museum, Dudley, West Midlands. At the time of writing in 2014, the trolleybus system was suspended until further notice; nevertheless, it has the longest length of route wiring.

North of England Open Air Museum, County Durham. Although there is overhead wiring in place, there is no active service in operation, though plans for an extension to a new projected village are underway.

For further studies of the trolleybus, we suggest two societies in particular: the National Trolleybus Society (www.trolleybus.co.uk/nta) and the British Trolleybus Society (www. britishtrolley.org.uk), dedicated to news at home and abroad and featuring interesting articles.

Acknowledgements

We wish to thank Fonthill Media for allowing us to fulfil a lifelong ambition—to chart the gradual demise of the British trolleybus in colour over this particular decade. All photographs were taken by ourselves. We have endeavoured to make sure all the facts are correct, however apologise in advance if, with the passing of time, some inaccuracies have crept in. We ask that the reader bear in mind that it is now over forty-three years since the last trolleybus disappeared off our roads.

Bibliography

Hyde, W. G. S., *History of Public Transport in Ashton* (Manchester: Manchester Transport Museum, 1980)

Maybin, Mike, *Nostalgic Look at Belfast Trolleybuses, 1938–68* (Kettering: Silver Link, 1997)

Fowler, David, *Bournemouth Trolleybuses* (London: Trolleybooks, 2001)

King, J. S., *Bradford Trolleybuses* (Venture Publishing, 1994)

Bowen and Callow, *Cardiff Trolleybuses* (London: National Trolleybus Association, 1969)

Doig, Alan C., and Craven, Maxwell, *Derby Trams & Buses* (Trent Valley Publications, 1986)

Bucley, Richard, *Trams and Trolleybuses in Doncaster* (Barnsley: Wharncliffe, 2003)

Brook, Roy, *Trolleybuses of Huddersfield* (Manchester: Manchester Transport Museum, 1976)

Wells, Malcolm, *Kingston upon Hull Trolleybuses* (London: Trolleybooks, 1996)

Barker, Colin, *Ipswich Trolleybuses* (Midhurst: Middleton Press, 2005)

Blacker, Ken, *London Trolleybuses*, vol. 1 (St Leonards-on-Sea: Capital Transport, 2002)

Eyre, Michael, and Heaps, Chris, *Manchester Trolleybuses* (Birmingham: Ian Allan, 2008)

Canneaux, T. P., and Hanson, N. H., *The Trolleybuses of Newcastle* (London: Trolleybooks, 1974)

Bowler, David, *Nottingham Trolleybuses* (London: Trolleybooks, 2006)

Hall, D. A., *Reading Trolleybuses* (London: Trolleybooks, 1991)

Burrows, G., *The Trolleybuses of South Shields* (London: Trolleybooks, 1976)

Challoner, Eric, *Trolleybus Memories Wolverhampton* (Birmingham: Ian Allan, 2007)

Harvey, David, *Walsall Trolleybuses* (Stroud: Amberley, 2009)

Joyce, J., King, J. C., and Newman, A. G., *British Trolleybus Systems* (Birmingham: Ian Allan, 1986)

Lockwood, Stephen, *Trackless to Trolleybus: Trolleybuses in Britain* (Fife: Adam Gordon, 2011)